# How to Watch a Baseball Game

*by Fred Schwed, Jr.*

_____

DRAWINGS BY LEO HERSHFIELD

# How to Watch a Baseball Game

*Harper & Brothers*

PUBLISHERS, NEW YORK

*This book is dedicated to that large
group of literate adults, women and men,
who are now "fans," but not quite real
fans. They are the people who once did
not care much about baseball, but whose interest has been aroused in the last decade
by their growing children's interest, or
by television, or by both.*

# Contents

# A Reverent Acknowledgment

At least half of the people over seven years old, living in North America, take a mild or avid interest in baseball and have been doing so for generations. Yet the amount of lyrical appreciation of this engrossing sport, or business, or religion, is incredibly small. Here is an all but complete catalogue dating from the turn of the century: One popular song, better than mediocre, "Take Me Out to the Ball Game;" and one excellent recitative comic poem, "Casey at the Bat." Compare this to the rhymed output on such subjects as mother love, regular

ix

love, football, and the more economically retarded areas of the Deep South or Ireland. I cannot explain why this is and neither can anyone in Tin Pan Alley, nor the editor of *Poetry*.

Fortunately the catalogue above is not quite complete. A dozen years ago, Rolfe Humphries, a fine and serious modern poet, wrote a fine and serious poem called "Polo Grounds." In some fifty magical lines it tells all that baseball ever was or will be.

I have used for chapter headings consecutive portions of the poem. This procedure smacks of being old fashioned but I like the idea, particularly since it insures that there will be something of value in the book.

I have also put the entire poem at the end of the book. This is out of consideration for those who like to read a good poem all in one piece as well as being randomly peppered with fragments of it.

F. S., Jr.

# How to Watch a Baseball Game

# CHAPTER ONE

# Baseball Semantics

---

*Time is of the essence. This is a highly skilled*
*And beautiful mystery.*

There are some people who know absolutely nothing about baseball. They not only cannot get to first base; they do not know where first base is.* However these people are almost entirely foreigners, but this does not apply to all foreigners. It does not apply to Canadians, Central Americans, or Japanese. It usually does not apply to foreigners who have had residence here for one full year, if

* It is to the right.

they have eager and curious minds.

It will therefore not be necessary to start right at the beginning, taking up which is the bat and which is the ball.

This is fortunate because baseball, which everyone understands so easily, cannot be explained to a complete beginner without taking him or her to a game, and pointing, as well as explaining. You can learn all you want to know about the bottom of the ocean by reading Miss Rachel Carson, but this will not work for baseball.

A case in point was related by Nunnally Johnson years and years before he became a Hollywood genius. The story was about a Chicago outfielder who fell in love with a New York chorus girl. He watched her on the stage every time he could, but for a long time he had no opportunity to allow her to see him play. Chicago only gets to New York eleven times a year. Among this player's other limitations was that he was only allowed to play against left-handed pitching. Left-handed pitching always seemed to occur on Wednesdays and Saturdays, when the girl of course had to play matinees.

Finally, however, love again laughed at locksmiths, and he was able to take her to a game in

which he was to play. He was in great excitement and it wasn't until the taxi had reached Ninetieth Street that he discovered that she had never seen a game and knew absolutely nothing about it. "Oh, my," he said, or words more or less to that effect, "that is terrible. If you don't understand the game you won't enjoy it. I'll explain it to you. The first guy gets up to take his cut. Maybe he whiffs, maybe he gets on. Let's say he gets on. So then there is a guy on first. Then the second guy comes up to take his cut. Maybe he whiffs, maybe he gets on. Let's say . . ."

The story went on from there, but she didn't seem to get much of a grasp on the game.

The other instance of explaining baseball I recall vividly. It was during the Second World War, well before the Normandy Invasion. I was in the employ of a propaganda agency initialed O.W.I. England was host to an army of American boys. England was happy to have them there but there were, naturally enough, various areas of misunderstanding. There is nothing like having a common language for permitting two nations to misunderstand each other. One of the minor irritants turned out to be baseball.

Our boys played a good deal of it among themselves and the British drifted about as spectators. Incomprehensibility ensued. This is always somewhat annoying, whether one is looking at a ball game, a cricket game, or a nonobjective painting. Meyer Berger of the *New York Times* filed a brief dispatch on this international situation:

He went to a game between two good GI teams and sat next to a father, a mother, and their several children. As the game progressed the kids began to get a good sprinkling of what was the general intent of all this mysterious activity. But their sire, it soon developed, did not. Halfway through the game the children were excitedly telling each other the principles they had pretty accurately picked up, when their father imperatively interrupted them.

"You've got it quite wrong," he told them. "The nub of the whole affair is those two chaps over there," and he pointed to a pitcher and catcher who were leisurely warming up on the sidelines.

I went to my superiors with the suggestion that a little booklet, with diagrams, should be created. It would be handed out gratis wherever baseball was played by Americans, and British were look-

ing on. It would not go into the profundities of the game. No, it would be simple and would start on the premise that these spectators, while they knew the bat from the ball, knew nothing else.

This seemed to me a simple and interesting assignment, but it turned out only to be interesting. I found this out immediately after slipping a piece of blank paper into the typewriter.

Have you ever tried to explain baseball, on paper, starting at the beginiing? Mind you, you can explain chemistry, starting at the beginning, and chemistry is a lot more complicated. But with baseball, where do you begin?

Do you start by describing the diamond (which does not resemble a diamond) or the number of innings (what is an inning, so different from the cricket inning?) or the stark fact that the team scoring the most runs wins? But what is a "run," how is it scored? And that leads us to how is it prevented. Well, by getting the batter or runner, or runners, "out." How are they put out? I discovered to my astonishment, while looking at a blank sheet of paper, scores of ways. And I had known this vast body of information, almost perfectly, since I was ten years old. So had millions of other Americans, many of them dumber than me. And we had all learned it without pain, effort, or study.

But probably you will be tempted to begin your exposition, as I at first was, with the real "nub of the whole affair." This is the continuing contest between the pitcher and catcher (not the ones warming up) and the succession of batters. This is appealing because it brings up in all its simple beauty the four balls, three strikes theorem. This beauty is of course immediately marred by third strike foul balls (all foul "balls" happen to be "strikes," except third strikes, which are neither unless they happen to be foul bunts); but that is another story, and as the expositor will find out, so is everything else in baseball.

Anyway, it eventually becomes evident that the four ball, three strike contest between pitcher and batter isn't the place to start explaining, whether it is the nub of the affair or not. You get parked on that dime, you have a hard time getting off it. What seemed to be a small matter turns out to be two and a half pages of the booklet.

It is perhaps best to begin by pointing out an anomaly, although an American just never thinks

*. . . there are no less than nine equally muscular men opposing him.*

of it as being one: When the first guy comes up to take his cut, he is all alone, and there are no less than nine equally muscular men opposing him. He has many comrades seated on the bench but the only help they can give him is oral, and rather limited at that. ("It only takes one to hit it, boy," and "That big bum ain't got nothing.")

How unusual this arrangement? Perhaps how unfair? In nearly all the other games of the world one contestant faces one contestant, or a team of two, or six, or fifteen faces a team of two or six or fifteen. The only important exceptions to this sportsmanlike arrangement are baseball, war, and cricket. In cricket two men face eleven. Thus it should be easier to explain baseball to an Englishman* than to a Spaniard (where a man faces one bull). Actually it is no easier at all, because while cricket seems to resemble baseball in a few aspects, the resemblance is superficial, and more likely to be misleading than helpful.

About the most knowledgeable non-American

* I recently discussed this matter with Mr. Charles Einstein, the well-known baseball reporter and editor, and he threw a little more light on it, or maybe darkness. It seems that a number of years ago another reporter took Fred Perry of England, then the best tennis player in the world, to his first American baseball game. Mr. Perry was suspicious of the whole affair, and when in the second inning the losing pitcher was shelled off the mound, and started his lugubrious trudge over second base and the outfield, Perry asked, "Where is *he* going?" The reporter said, "To the showers." "It's a hot day," said Perry, "I imagine he will feel famously when he comes back."

fan I ever saw a ball game with is a Frenchman who came to this country when he was thirty years old. They do many things in France but they don't play either cricket or baseball. He brought a completely blank mind to the game. He was fascinated; he studied hard; in record time he won his Phi Beta Kappa key in the American madness.

Yet all American children enter high school knowing more about it than he did when he graduated. Let us inquire into this miracle.

# CHAPTER TWO

# How to Watch a Baseball Game

*Three or four seconds only*
*From the time that Riggs connects till he reaches first,*
*And in those seconds Jurges goes to his right,*
*Comes up with the ball, tosses to Witek at second*
*For the force on Reese, Witek to Mize at first,*
*In time for the out—a double play.*

When we speak of how to watch a baseball game the first thing to consider is which baseball game to watch on that particular day or night. Your personal geography will enter strongly into this. The very best game to watch is clearly a big-

*... very minor ball will be most enjoyed by fathers,
mothers, sweethearts, ...*

league affair, preferably between the team that is leading its particular big league and the one in second place, with both managers "going" with their best pitchers. However if you happen to be residing on the banks of the Rio Grande this presents some obvious difficulties and you may have to settle for some less highly skilled and less beautiful mystery.

Let's face it, this is too bad. Baseball, unlike many other exhibitions, such as wrestling, is only entrancing when it is played by the best three or four hundred players in the world. (There are a few occasions when it is punk even then.) Baseball resembles violin playing; it is a dubious privilege to listen to someone playing the violin fairly well. Frankly, high school, college, and sandlot, and very minor ball will be most enjoyed by fathers, mothers, sweethearts, and brides of the players, plus a sprinkling of other relatives, pals, siblings, and personal adorers. However all these good people will enjoy the game and so will some others, those who like to see action whether it is skillful professional action or not.

If, like most fans, you are not even acquainted with any of baseball's personable young men, settle if possible for something like a Giants-Dodgers conflict on the Fourth of July. The chances are this will be the most rewarding, although you cannot be as sure as when you pick a play, a movie, or a sermon.

A favorite subject for scholarly discussion is where to sit, once in the park, presuming you have the choice. Some say behind first base, where most of the action should occur, some behind third where most of the illegal betting occurs; and some plump for the bleachers, so democratic, so economical, so sunny. A child, male, wants to sit in the upper tier where he will have a chance to try to catch a foul fly. Fortunately his chances for this opportunity are astronomically against him.

The chief point to bear in mind if it is a big game which you and yours very much want to see is to get into the ball park. This can be accomplished by getting tickets in advance or by getting there early enough. The worst seat in the stands, behind a post or in front of a paranoiac, is better than being turned away because all the seats have been sold. I happen to know this because on more than one occason I have had this calamity happen to me.

So now you are in your seat. The national an-

*. . . in front of a paranoiac, is better than
being turned away . . .*

them, the warm-up pitches, the first man up, usually a fast little guy. Isn't it exciting? Who knows
what will happen? Maybe a long succession of
foul balls. Never mind, something different will
happen after that; in a century of play it always has.

Now face forward and pay as strict attention as

your attention paying equipment will allow you to do. If you don't know much about it, ask questions. If you know all about it give little lectures. If you only think you know all about it give little lectures anyway. You are in a sense touching elbows with tens of thousands of your neighbors. They have all of them (except a few in the press box) one pleasant thing in common. They came to have a good time, not to improve themselves. Join with them. Be alternately adoring and derisive. Don't forget to stand up in your team's turn in the seventh inning, and be sure not to fall asleep.

# CHAPTER THREE

# The Crowd

*(Red Barber crescendo. Crowd noises, obbligato;*
*Scattered staccatos from the peanut boys,*
*Loud in the lull, as the teams are changing sides)* . . .

*Hubbell takes the sign, nods, pumps, delivers—*
*A foul into the stands. Dunn\* takes a new ball out,*
*Hands it to Danning, who throws it down to Werber;*
*Werber takes off his glove, rubs the ball briefly,*
*Tosses it over to Hub, who goes to the rosin bag,*
*Takes the sign from Danning, pumps, delivers—*

\* For the benefit of the younger generation, Dunn was an umpire.

*Low, outside, ball three. Danning goes to the mound,*
*Says something to Hub, Dunn brushes off the plate,*
*Adams starts throwing in the Giant bullpen,*
*Hub takes the sign from Danning, pumps, delivers,*
*Camilli gets hold of it, a* long *fly to the outfield,*
*Ott goes back, back, back, against the wall, gets*
    *under it,*
*Pounds his glove, and takes it for the out.*
*That's all for the Dodgers. . . .*

*Time is of the essence.*

There are, at any given moment, eighteen players participating in a ball game, plus two managers, two coaches, two batboys, and four umpires. That makes twenty-six. There is a twenty-seventh human entity present. That is "the crowd."

It is valid to argue that the crowd is an important single entity at a ball game. The crowd may consist, say, of forty-thousand eyes and twenty-thousand noses, all of them different, and there are always some rooters *against* the home team. But the crowd is a single emotional voice, sometimes triumphant, sometimes furious, sometimes half asleep. After a good game a fan comes away with the satisfactory feeling that he has taken a personal part in a large human demonstration. The crowd, even a small one, is important for the real enjoyment of the game. One of the many flaws of television baseball is that the "crowd" is too small, often consisting of just you. The disembodied yowling of a distant throng, which the announcer permits you to hear at his discretion, is not convincing. There are no interesting strangers at your elbows.

There is an analogy here between the theater and baseball, although the theater is several thousand years older. When I was in college I took a peculiar course called Dramatic Technique. The course must have had merit because I still remember the opening session perfectly and that session was not day before yesterday. The professor asked the class to give a definition of a "play." We all stumbled around and proposed definitions. None of them was right, which is not surprising because the professor had invented his own definition, which I still think was a good one.

"A play," he finally revealed, "is not yet a play if it only exists in manuscript, or if it is officially published in book form with all the 'sides' and stage directions. A play is a play only when it is

performed by actors before an audience. Even
then it often is not yet a play. A dress rehearsal is
not a play. A performance given before an audience
consisting of the relatives and friends of the actors
and the playwright is not a play. It does not come
up to the acid test of a real performance. It is not
a play if it is a run-through for half a dozen visiting
nabobs from Hollywood. That may be important,
but it is not a play.

"A play is a formal dramatic presentation on a
real stage before a real audience. A real audience
is composed of a number of persons, nearly all of
them strangers to the cast and management, who
have of their own free will, and not for some
worthy cause, paid money for a ticket. The only
ones in the audience who have not paid money will
be such professional critics as may be present and
the two or three firemen who in some cities are re-
quired to be present.

"I see that some of you look skeptical about this
definition but I hope to persuade you that the definition is sound. A real play does not exist 'in
camera.' A real play is a shared emotional experience. It is shared by the cast and the audience and
also shared by the members of the audience them-

selves. If the woman just in front of you is laughing or weeping, it will help your evening more than if she is yawning. If Noel Coward's most brilliant comedy were presented by a fine cast in a theater in the Ozarks, and one of you sophisticated young men attended, I assure you that you would not enjoy it, surrounded by an audience that found the play incomprehensible, or ridiculous, or dirty. In the same vein, I do not remember that an enormously popular play, *Uncle Tom's Cabin*, seriously performed, was ever any sort of success on Broadway, in New York City. Or in Biloxi, either, come to think about it. Thank you for your attention. Class dismissed."

The crowd at the ball game is different from all other crowds. Not "better," just different. At tennis and golf the crowd is silent, at the races the crowd only wakes up seven or eight times all afternoon for one or two hundred furious seconds. The football people are expensively dressed and many of them are tipsy. The fight mob is mostly inexpensively dressed and some of them are criminals. The audience at court tennis is impeccable but very limited.

Let us not claim too much for the fans at the

ball park but let us salute them and give them their duc. I have never seen anyone take a snort out of a flask at a ball game, but undoubtedly it is done. I have never seen in a ball park the brutality of a fight crowd, but very occasionally I have seen something approaching it. I have never actually witnessed a fist fight in the stands although I have often seen that one was taking place two hundred yards away; everybody in between stands up and few are the witnesses who can testify who was fighting or what in all creation they were fighting about. At least once there was a murder in the stands. Murderer and victim were strangers to one another. If enough ball games are played, every so often something wonderful will happen. By the same token, if you play enough games before enough millions of people something horrible will, but very rarely, happen. In any crowd of five or twenty thousand persons, several of them will be insane. No two of these should ever be seated together, but there is no way to arrange against this.

But game by game for a thousand games, spectator by spectator for a million fans, baseball, and baseball watching, is a delightful element in our life in the U.S.A. It compares favorably with small boat sailing and is more convenient and less expensive. It is clearly superior to holiday motoring and is much less conducive to sudden death.

The ball crowds are almost unanimously eager, knowledgeable, and friendly. Strangers seated together do not as a rule murder each other. What they usually do is to form gay companionships, lasting about two hours. These friendships are scarcely ever resumed. It is perhaps because of this that they are unembarrassed and rewarding. Some authorities say that illness is not the major disaster of our time, but that loneliness is. Nobody needs to be lonely in a grandstand. All you need to do for an introduction is to hear one of your neighbors voice an opinion. Then say to him, "You nuts?" But say it politely.

The next matter up for consideration is an important one—kids, with the emphasis on male kids. The first thrill a father gets from a first son is to view him as a newborn infant. This marks the first time he ever viewed an infant with enthusiasm unmarred by hypocrisy. His second, third, and fourth thrills vary according to temperament and circumstances. But if the father is a fan, one of the things he is looking forward to is taking the boy out to

*"You nuts?"*

the old ball game. He plans when it will be proper to do this, and invariably he does it a bit too early. But no great harm is done.

I guess my boy was about six when I took him to the Polo Grounds. We emerged from a tunnel and the shaver saw for the first time the meticulously manicured infield and outfield. He stopped short and breathed, "Grass. Green grass!" His face was radiant at this lovely surprise, and then I saw he was patting his palms together. He was applauding the grass, in a quiet way. And for my part, I was enchanted.

Of course by the end of the third, when the game hadn't even become legal yet, he was bored stiff. His interest in the vendors of comestibles was greater than his interest in Rogers Hornsby from the very beginning. By the third, he was no longer interested in the vendors.

The moral of all this is: Take your little boy, or even your little girl, to the game, but only if you are willing to leave before it is over. Baseball is an intellectual exercise, and the little ones won't comprehend it unless they are little Mozarts.

However, some years later take the tykes and stay for the whole nine innings, or even fourteen. There is no friendlier way for a father to spend time with his son.* The emotional complications that involve so many fathers and sons can, in a grandstand, be all projected forward, toward the game, instead of sideways. The precise moment of maturity, when your son will be eager to view the ball game as a ball game, rather than a haphazard picnic, is easily stated. It is the moment he learns to do "long division" accurately. That is the mo-

* This is Doctor Spock's janitor speaking.

ment when his intellect has arrived at the comprehension of baseball; and all baseball percentages are arrived at by long division.

There is a belief that our national game makes for morality in the young. If they worship ball players they are not so liable to throw rocks through the windows of passing trains. I have a feeling that there is truth in this, but I certainly cannot prove it, nor can the newspaper writers and others who proffer the idea steadily. Did any scientist ever go through the penitentaries asking the prisoners whether they were interested in baseball when they were young? Here is a project for some foundation interested in projects.

This matter of morality brings up an awful thing that once happened in baseball. It is also a fascinating thing. In the life of Jesus, the role of Judas is not admirable, but it is interesting.

I am referring of course to the Black Sox scandal in the World Series of 1919. This event has always seemed to me at least as provocative of speculative thought as the Battle of the Coral Sea, where the ships never sighted one another. In the 1919 Series nobody sighted anybody. Eight of the Chicago American Leaguers didn't even sight themselves.

Over the years I have talked with a number of old-timers who claim they know what happened. To believe it at all, or even some of it, you have to keep in mind firmly the unpredictability of young athletic males.

Let us admit that in 1919 ball players were not paid so well as they were a short time later. However they were still a lot better paid than ribbon clerks, and even if they hadn't been their careers were more thrilling. So this seems to be about what happened:

The Chicago White Sox, later to be referred to as the Black Sox, were one of the all-time great teams. Both the fans and the gamblers figured that they ought to be able to win easily enough over the Cincinnati Reds, particularly in a nine-game series. (It was a nine-game series that time which is a rather grubby item in itself. Interest was high, so the powers that were, figured they could sell out the stands for such an unwieldy series.)

Gamblers delicately approached eight members of the Chicago club. They selected the eight who held the highest averages in ignorance and greed. The two foremost, if that is the right word, of the eight were Shoeless Joe Jackson, the great hitting

*Gamblers delicately approached eight members . . .*

outfielder, and Eddie Cicotte, the great pitcher. By this time Jackson should be in Baseball's Hall of Fame in Cooperstown, instead of wherever he is, God help him. Jackson could not read or write; Cicotte, and the six others, obviously couldn't think.

The winning team got more than a thousand dollars apiece more than the losing team, so the gamblers offered to put several thousand dollars under the pillows of the eight chosen young men if they lost. All eight thought that this was a real brainy idea. Just how many thousands were offered has not been exactly established, but this does not matter.

What does matter is that after the eight players had scrupulously lost the series five games to three, nobody, not even the hotel chambermaid, left anything under their pillows.

When this happened, it conjures up a picture worth conjuring. These eight panicked stupid, ball players of excellence held their secret meetings. They were all shortly to be disgraced and deprived of their fame and their salaries. The immediate question was of course to whom could they appeal to get their earned money? The cops, President Woodrow Wilson, or the Prince of Darkness, or Arnold Rothstein? It was a question they had never considered before.

When the case finally broke open some months later, it was all quite wonderful in a horrible sort of way. Cicotte testified tearfully that he did it "for the wife and kiddies." How the wife and kiddies fared is a bit of research I would not care to undertake. Shoeless Joe Jackson was thrown out of baseball with the rest, although he batted the best in that series, a percentage of .375. It is likely that poor Joe never did much understand what it was all about. All he ever knew for sure was how to step into a good pitch with grace and power. This is not to suggest that he should have been forgiven for accepting a bribe that he never got and also never properly earned.

One of the greatest American expressions stems from Jackson's peculiar martyrdom. It is reported that at the courthouse steps a newsboy, blubbering, called out, "Say it ain't so, Joe."

Why did these eight grown men arrange to do this childish, hopeless, and suicidal thing? I have long given it a good deal of thought and I have come up with a possible answer.

The answer concerns the difficult relations between businessmen and artists. Big-league ball players are clearly artists, not businessmen. They perform an aesthetic function and they can prove it more clearly than many an abstract painter, for instance. They can perform their artistry so well that there are only four hundred of them at a given time. There is no margin of doubt as to which four hundred they are; they get their names in the paper nearly every day.

I have spent half my life with businessmen and half with artists, and I have observed a funny thing. Most businessmen would like to prove that they could be artists if they tried. So they make complicated furniture in the basement, they watercolor, they work in amateur theatricals, they compose comical songs and skits for birthday parties, and when they meet a writer they confide to him that they could a tale unfold if only the writer would sit down and polish it off.

But the artists envy businessmen. To be more accurate, they envy them and despise them at the same time, which leads to a schizophrenic state of mind. The artist* feels that the businessmen receive vast amounts of money, not by doing any hard work, but by stealing the money in some secret and complex fashion. They strongly disapprove of this but they can't help hankering to try the same thing. I have heard some artists, in their leisure hours, discussing common stocks and convertible debentures in quiet, serious gibberish, like small children playing house.

So here is the suggested answer as to why the Black Sox did it. They didn't want to disgrace the

* Some artists even buy baseball teams, usually bum ones.

National Pastime; they did not plan to disillusion the youth of our nation. They just wanted to be wise guys, like the men in the double-breasted suits who sit in the first-row boxes. The gamblers took them aside and said out of the corner of their cigar, "Wise up, son, wise up." So they were quickly persuaded. These were the same gamblers who couldn't have persuaded a milkmaid to give them a kiss.

The personality of crowds varies from city to city. In New York, an international type city, a large slice of the audience is rooting for the *visiting* team. This does not happen in Milwaukee. Does it happen in San Francisco? One would think so. I don't happen to know. In the City of Brotherly Love the fans occasionally act so abominably that fans in other cities are tempted to hand in their resignation card to the human race. Boston also can be sometimes awful, almost always toward its greatest performer, Ted Williams. Why the head shrinkers don't take time off to look into this I also don't know. But in Cincinnati—well allow me to tell you a minor detail about Cincinnati, home of the Redlegs, an aggregation which over the years has not done particularly well.

What I am about to divulge about Cincinnati is not at all exciting (maybe you know it already but I doubt it). It is only related to illustrate a point: That a moderately intelligent fan can go all his life and still learn something every month or so that he didn't know before about baseball. This is the sort of situation that helps keep middle-aged people from becoming old people. It is true of many other pursuits, such as life, love, literature, or trading in precious stones.

It took this moderately intelligent fan some twenty years before he discovered the detail about Cincinnati. The opening day of the season, in the middle of April, is always a good day for attendance in all the cities. Thus, clubs swap opening days.

However, at Cincinnati the first game is *always* played there. This is because the citizens of this Ohio city do not consider Opening Day just as Opening Day. They consider it one small notch below Christmas. The park is always sold out; the offices are shut; the thousands who can't get in the park go home to their radios and TV sets to pray and meditate. There are more religions than are listed under the heading "Religions" in the encyclopedia.

Opening games are of course a part of the regular 154-game series. But World Series games and all-star games* are not. The hits, errors, and other statistics are kept in a separate file and are not often consulted. The crowds that almost always fill the stands are different from the crowds of the regular season. They are more prosperous; they have to be to buy tickets. Some of them want to see and some of them want to be seen. They do not understand or love baseball so well as some crowd of four thousand on a muggy day in August. Why should they? Many of them came, not because it was a ball game, but because it was an enormously publicized event. A comparison can be made with an evening dress first-night crowd at the theater and a Saturday matinee crowd months later. The matinee bunch bought their cheap tickets purely because they wanted to see the show and the actors and actresses. They had no illusions about personal publicity. They had no expectations, as in Morris Bishop's

---

*In all-star games the players are chosen by balloting. Millions of fans vote. It is Democracy at its most transcendent. All the voters get out of it is the loss of a three-cent stamp or a two-cent postal card. Dishonesty in counting the votes has never been charged.

*. . . instinctive dislikers of graceful success.*

happy phrase, "to be merry as a draper with his picture in the paper."

There is one crowd that cannot precisely be called a baseball "crowd." Though they often attend at the same park, no park is large enough to house a fraction of one per cent of them. They are not so much a crowd as a state of mind. They are the instinctive dislikers of graceful success. I estimate their number as 14,170,222. They are the Yankee Haters.

For the past quarter century the New York team of the American League has done so much better than any of its sometimes changing fifteen rivals that it is shocking to many minds. Money, it is often charged, is the answer to this; they have money and they make money, and they buy up all the best players. However there are other clubs that have money, and don't make money, and don't win pennants and world championships with infuriating regularity. Worse than that, the Yankees do it with aristocratic detachment; no unseemly episodes, no brainstorms or scandals. Baseball reporters have told me that when the Yankee front office considers a player they think of his hitting, his defensive work, his speed of foot, *and* his personality pattern. Thus there are few, if any, personality disasters, which sometimes plague lesser clubs. Come to think of it, the last personality problem the Yankees had was Babe Ruth, who single handed built their marvelous stadium for them.

The Yankees have many loyal fans, who spend

*. . . a sort of*

most of their summers in sleek satisfaction, watching their favorites romp home by several lengths. The Yankee Haters spend most of their summers drinking a bitter brew.

*capricious patriotism.*

Intense partisanship—personal loving identification with a team or a single player, or sometimes with hate of a great player like Ted Williams—is a subject with fascination. Unfortunately, few philosophers are ball fans, so this is mostly virgin speculative territory. A sort of patriotism seems to be at the heart of it. However, the patriotism is a sort of capricious patriotism. The citizens of New York, Northern New Jersey, and Southern Connecticut and Western Long Island have three big-league teams to adore—Yankees, Giants, and Bums. In all cases each citizen (*and he cannot tell you why*) adores one and despises the other two. I know of one citizen of New York City who despises all three of them and adores the Pittsburgh Pirates, an unrewarding vigil. The best explanation of all this can be found in Proverbs, XXX, 19: "The way of an eagle in the air; the way of a serpent upon a rock; the way of a ship in the midst of the sea; and the way of a man with a maid." To this could at this date be added the way of a fan with a big-league club.

All this is further complicated by the fact, hidden from nobody, that the idolized players of the Yankees rarely come from the Bronx and the idolized players of Kansas City never come from Kansas City (so far). Furthermore they are often "traded," and when your favorite player, like Maglie, moves over from the esteemed Giants to the abominable

Brooklyns, a fan has a tough emotional decision to make. This brings up a related subject. The subject is "trading."

A few years ago, and let us pray it never happens again, our country was riven on the subject of which Americans were Communists or fellow travelers. An incredible amount of energy and money and hatred was expended trying to determine this. I had my own method, which was at least inexpensive and quick. Just say to the suspect something about baseball. If he says something moderately sensible about the pennant race, we clear him. But if his first remark is, "Baseball, that is the game where they sell players down the river, like Negro slaves before the Civil War," in that case we must take another look.

Where did he get his silly idea? He didn't make it up all by himself. He got it from a friend of a friend of a friend who got it from Moscow which is a famous factory for silly ideas. It is true that players are traded not only up and down the river but often sideways. The analogy however is entertainingly faulty. Negro slaves before the Civil War did not start practicing to be slaves at the age of seven, did not pray beside their little beds that they would some day make the grade (they nearly always did), and when they made the grade they were not guaranteed a minimum salary of $6000 a year plus free large meals, expensive accommodations, and maybe pictures of themselves on the TV, shaving, with a safety razor, for a large fee.

# CHAPTER FOUR

# Concerning Hurry

---

*The rhythms break,*
*More varied and subtle than any kind of dance;*
*Movement speeds up or lags. The ball goes out*
*In sharp and angular drives, or long, slow arcs,*
*Comes in again controlled and under aim;*
*The players wheel or spurt, race, stoop, slide, halt,*
*Shift imperceptibly to new positions,*
*Watching the signs, according to the batter,*
*The score, the inning. Time is of the essence.*

The various details about baseball, according to the last census, amount to 10,051. I do not know

*"The players wheel or spurt, race, stoop, slide, halt . . ."*

all of them and this is fortunate for everybody
concerned.

Consider the Official Rules. They resemble a
volume of Blackstone's *Commentaries* on law. They

are divided into ten divisions, and each division has many rules. Thus the first rule is number 1.01 and makes for rather unrewarding study:

"1.01. BASEBALL is a game between two teams of nine players each with adequate substitutes, under direction of a Manager, played in accordance with these rules, under an umpire or umpires on an enclosed field."

The next rule is the most important one of the lot and thus might be termed the Golden Rule of Baseball, although it never has been:

"1.02. THE OBJECT of each team is to win by scoring more runs than the opponent."

We now skip a hundred or so rules and come to rule 7.09 (i) which is put in nomination as the least important one. It is generally referred to as "the 45-foot rule," but it is generally not referred to at all.

Have you ever noticed an apparently meaningless white line, three feet away and parallel to the first base line, and beginning, mystically, halfway to first base and stopping three feet on the outside of first base? Most fans have seen hundreds of games without bothering their pretty heads about that. The third base line is not so embellished.

"7.09 (i). It is interference by a batter or a runner when—(i) in running the last half of the distance from home base to first base while the ball is being fielded to first base, he runs outside (to the right of) the three foot line, or inside (to the left of) the foul line and, in the umpire's judgment, interferes with the fielder taking the throw at first base, or attempting to field a batted ball."

Putting it another way, if the bum does this the bum is out, unless the umpire has a particular fondness for him, which is a rarity.

Official Rules aside, here is the most important thing to keep in your consciousness when you are watching a baseball game, or when you are thinking about baseball in bed, just before falling asleep, as I have discovered a surprising number of people do. It is the delicate arrangement of time and distance, unequaled in any other game. The distance between home plate and first is ninety feet. It requires, as our poet has more musically pointed out, a right-handed batter about three and a half seconds to run to first. It would require him a tiny bit less if he were left-handed. It usually requires a shortstop or third baseman a little bit less than three and a half seconds to perform his part of the ballet on

*. . . another split decision . . .*

a ground ball. Sometimes it requires him a little bit more. Then the guy is safe. Sometimes, such is the unmerciful hurry of most baseball plays, the infielder "throws the ball away." Throwing the ball away is an unforgiveable error. It means throwing it as far from the first baseman as you or I would do if we got the opportunity to perform before thousands. (You never see an infielder do that in infield practice, which is so much more leisurely.) When this tragedy occurs, the curtain is not rung down. The runner probably decides to try for second (he has a grace note of time to mull this matter over.) Various fielders scamper, one retrieves the ball as it bounces off concrete, and then in another few seconds there is likely to be another split decision, full of dust, at second base.

It is true that the runner, during his little moment of indecision, is privileged to engage the experienced advice of his first base coach, who is usually a gray-haired Nestor, and besides has a better and more objective view of the situation. Just so do big businessmen consult their attorneys, save that the difference in time is enormous. Sometimes a big star, or an emotional rookie, disregards the coach's shouted advice, and sometimes he is right and sometimes he is very wrong.

The play recently described, a grounder hit to the shortstop or third baseman, is the game's classic play. And it is always a hairline decision. Well, not quite always. If the runner is a lugubriously slow runner, the decision may not be close. However such slow runners do not get jobs in big league baseball, unless they happen to be fabulous hitters, or wonderful catchers, or fairly good pitchers.

A ball hit to the second baseman may be a routine play, but often it is nothing of the kind. A ball fielded cleanly by the pitcher is just a nothing play; the pitcher has eternity to throw the runner out at first and an experienced pitcher takes a little less than eternity to do it.

Consider a few other classic plays, all of them hairline. There is the steal of second base. The stealer has to run ninety feet, less a few precious feet that constitute his "lead." That of course is why the pitcher so often wheels and throws, fruitlessly, to first. This seems to some of the spectators a boring delay. He never gets the stealer out doing that. (Well, once in a long while he does. Once in a long while everything imaginable happens in baseball, a mathematical matter we shall examine later.) The pitcher himself is not sanguine about getting the stealer out with his many throws to first. What he is doing is to cut the stealer's lead down by a foot or two. That is likely to spell all the difference a few moments later. The catcher and the second baseman, or shortstop, if they each perform perfectly, will get the stealer out at second base, not at first. Incidentally, if they don't get him out, it is quite likely to be the pitcher's fault. A pitcher is a man faced with a sea of troubles. Just one of them is that when there is a fast man on first, he must not merely pitch the ball well, he must pitch it in a hurry. Good base stealers often say that they steal on the pitcher, not the catcher.

But when it comes to hairline plays, I will now describe one which, in my infinite wisdom, I deem to be impossible to perform. This is odd, because with my own two eyes I have seen it performed a few score times:

It is late in the game and the score is tied. The first guy up hits a double. Now the opposition, it is admitted, knows that the second guy up is going to try to bunt. So does everyone else present except a little boy who at the moment is more interested in going to the bathroom.

If the batter manages to bunt with any small degree of skill, I do  not see how it is possible to throw out the runner at third. At second he can take a little longer lead than if he were at first, because he is directly behind the pitcher's back. He is tentatively off on his eighty-three-foot journey before he hears the click of the bunt, and then he is

hurtling. The little bunt goes dribbling along, somewhere between the pitcher and either foul line.
There are four players who may handle this impossible assignment. The first problem is, which
one of them? This has to be decided, but immediately. The second problem is, the duly elected
candidate for this duty must get to the ball, which
is bumbling about slowly, reach down, pick it up,
turn almost entirely around and fire it to third
base. The third baseman must now "tag"* the man
out, for there is no forceout in this situation. He
must tag the man out, and he is facing away from
the man as he catches the throw. The man in ques-
ton is approaching him like a tornado with spikes

---

* "Tag" means the fielder must slap the ball on the runner
(sometimes painfully) before the runner reaches the sanctu-
ary of a foot on the base. It is a much more difficult play
for the infielder to make, since the runner slides, than the
"forceout." On the forceout the infielder just steps on the
bag and disdains even glancing at the runner. It is always a
forceout at first base. It is also a forceout when there are men
on the bases immediately behind any runner. The legal principle is that if a runner has no choice save to proceed forward,
he can be put out without being tagged. When and how this
delicate principle was introduced I have been unable to
discover, but must note that it makes the game more interesting.

*The man in question is approaching him*

hooked on the front, and in the moment in question
is about a yard away.

I hope I have made it clear that in this situation
it is impossible to keep the runner from advancing

*like a tornado . . .*

to third, as any intelligent person can clearly see,
if the batter produces any kind of acceptable bunt,
at all, at all. The only possible shred of evidence
against this theory is that the runner is not in-

frequently thrown out by a crack infield.

I will try to explain how this little miracle is performed without really believing that it has ever been performed.

It is obvious that there is going to be a bunt attempt, because that should move the runner on second to third. True, if the defense chooses the sensible action, they can throw out the bunter easily enough at first. But that leaves a man on third, with only one out. A man in this position ought to be able to score one important run before two more outs are made if he just doesn't get stomach cramps.

At the pitch, the first baseman and the pitcher leave their proper positions and rush at the batter as though they were going to tackle him. This is not just good tactics; it is high courage. If the batter decides at the last moment that he will not lay down the classic bunt, but take a slug at the ball, he is liable to have the satisfaction of knocking somebody's head off, something like David and Goliath. However he probably bunts, unless he does not mind having some coolness between himself and his manager. He slides his upper hand almost halfway up the bat, and in effect tries to stop the ball with that hand, which should not be difficult, but would be painful if done. However he just misses the ball with his hand and thus just taps it with the part of the bat that is next to his hand. A big leaguer ought to be able to do this unless he is a big-league pitcher. A pitcher is often just a throwing machine, sometimes incapable of, and occasionally uninterested in, performing anything else on a baseball diamond but throwing.

The infielder who somehow procures the ball promptly must give another split second to look about and see how everything is coming, especially the man coming into third. He must then make up his mind—the easy play at first (the second baseman is covering that bag) or the impossible one at third? If he tries the impossible one and it turns out to be impossible, the situation is as follows: The score is still tied, there are runners at third *and* first, *nobody* is out. Also the pitcher is in a frame of mind that none of his comrades can deal with. That is, unless it was the pitcher himself who threw to third, and in this case they had better bring a psychiatrist out to deal with him.

Let's say the miracle is not successfully performed, for a change, and there *is* a guy on first and third and nobody out. But the pitcher pulls himself

*. . . keeping one eye on the outfielder*

together and bears down (he'd better) so the next guy whiffs. Now we have another beautiful situation. Let's go the whole imaginative hog and say it is the last of the ninth inning, or the seventeenth. If the pitcher can get the next bum out, without a run coming in, there will be two outs, and then from this nightmare inning the odds will have changed to the probability of no score that inning.

*and the other eye on the runner's right heel . . .*

But if the bum can now just manage to lift an ordinary fly ball to the outfield, a fly easy to catch, then the audience will have about eight seconds of the stuff that dreams are made on. The outfielder who waits under the fly, a moderate one, will await it with a beating heart. He will angle his body so his throwing arm is toward the fence behind him. The man on third will "tag up" like a sprinter at the mark, which is suddenly what he has become. The third-base umpire will be performing the feat of keeping one eye on the outfielder and the other eye on the runner's right heel, which must remain touching the base until the instant the ball is caught.

There will then promptly ensue a remarkable short race. It will be between a man running an entire ninety feet as though the hounds of hell were after him and a thrown baseball traveling more than two hundred feet. Of course if the ball is not thrown accurately to the waiting catcher, it is no race, and that ball game is over. But suppose it is thrown accurately, as it usually is. (Who will win? Tune in again next Monday and find out.)

Actually the above scene is not so imaginative. I happened to see a World Series game in the mid-1930s and I have never forgotten its last play. It was between the Giants and the Yankees; it was the tenth inning; Moore of the Giants, a fast runner, was on third, and there was one out. There was a huge roar when Bill Terry, then manager, came out of the dugout as a pinch hitter. Terry was then widely disliked but he was no bum. He had a terrible knee at that time. But his object, and he was one of the greatest of batters, was to hit at least a respecta-

ble fly to the outfield. After that he could proceed
to first base in a wheelchair so far as anybody but
Mrs. Terry was concerned. I never saw whether he
ran or limped or swooned in pain; I had other things
to look at. So did everybody else present.

I will not pretend to remember which pitch it
was, but finally the ineffable Terry got hold of a
piece of the ball, not such a big piece, and raised a
lazy fly between left and center, somewhat more
to left than center. But the Yankee left fielder, who-
ever he was, politely refrained from catching it.
Joe DiMaggio, the center fielder, raced over as only
he could race. He caught the ball easily enough
but he was racing west as though he wanted to go
back to San Francisco. It took him several strides
to pull up, wheel, and throw. Moore scored, the
game was over, and I won thirty-two dollars. What
an idyllic early autumn afternoon that was.

It wasn't until I was in bed that night, drowsily
ruminating, that it dawned on me what was unusual
about that play. The Yankees had decided that if
Terry hit one, the arm that returned the ball to
the plate should be the arm of Joe DiMaggio, if
this were in any way practicable. It wasn't.

The dimensions of a baseball diamond are so

perfect that most of the plays are thrilling. A baseball diamond is as rigidly constructed as a tennis court.* The arrangement of the bases, and the pitcher's mound, is a thing of beauty. It has lasted nearly a century and should be a thing of joy forever. But that is not the complete reason why most plays are close plays. The diamond was conceived by Major Abner Doubleday before his part in the Civil War and later perfected by Cartwright, it is said. But the inner reason why most of the plays are close is the wisdom, experience, hopes, and fears of topnotch players.

A defensive player on the field wishes to play as far away from the batter as he can. This will lessen the chances of his getting his head knocked off, and will permit him to handle his fielding chances more cleanly and with more leisure. But a good player does not play back; he plays *in*, just as far as he dares. If there is a slow man at bat the infield men

---

* However, the outfield fences are almost as randomly constructed as a golf course. ("Random" is sometimes not the proper word. For example, the right-field foul line in Yankee Stadium is scandalously short. It helped Babe Ruth, a lefthanded flailer, to knock in many homers. That short "fence" was constructed thoughtfully; no one can estimate how many million dollars its few yards of shortness brought into the till.

can play back, but if there is a fast runner at bat, they must play closer by a yard or they won't throw him out.

That is why you often see close plays against even a slow man. That is why a great outfielder plays in closer than an ordinary outfielder. If the ball is hit into short outfield he can catch it. But if it is hit over his head, the great outfielder turns his back on the soaring ball and races toward the fence. As he does this he keeps his eye on the ball, an eye he seems to have on the back of his head and under his cap. At just the right moment he turns to the tumult and catches the ball. An ordinary outfielder plays a few yards farther back. When a single is sliced in well in front of him, only the cognoscenti make a mental note that Willie Mays, or Duke Snider, would have been playing closer in.

An interesting example of this sort of defensive adjustment is the play last described. On that one, the Yankee outfield was playing unusually close for a powerful batter like Terry. True, he might bust one way over their heads. But what is the sense of making arrangements to catch a fly somewhere near the fence with Joe Moore waiting at third with the winning run? Anybody might make the catch, but no one in the world could throw Moore out at the plate from that distance.

Baseball is one of the most romantic and sentimental of games. But in many of its aspects it is, and must be, coldly realistic.

# CHAPTER FIVE

# Statistics: The Wonderful versus the Probable

*Time is of the essence. Remember Terry?*
*Remember Stonewall Jackson, Lindstrom, Frisch,*
*When they were good? Remember Long George*
    *Kelly?*
*Remember John McGraw and Benny Kauff?*
*Remember Bridwell, Tenney, Merkle, Youngs,*
*Chief Meyers, Big Jeff Tesreau, Shufflin' Phil?*
*Remember Mathewson, and Ames, and Donlin,*
*Buck Ewing, Rusie, Smiling Mickey Welch?*

*Remember a left-handed catcher named Jack*
    *Humphries,\**
*Who sometimes played the outfield, in '83?*

The official box scores are the basic material for baseball's endless statistics or "records." Many of them are fascinating and some of them are boring, or even annoying, as we shall see later. It is safe to say that no other outdoor sport is so rich for the arithmetic-minded historian, not even golf.

A very indoor sport is the only superior to baseball in brief historical accuracy. That one is chess. The report of a chess game takes no more space than a box score and tells a lot more. A decent chess player today can have a book at his elbow and re-play a game, with all its subtleties and thrills, that Paul Morphy played a century ago, a long time before his death and shortly before he went mad.

There is an analogy between a classic, low-scoring ball game, and a classic chess game. The two managers, say Paul Richards and Casey Stengel,

---

\* John Henry Humphries, like all the others mentioned in this stanza, played for the Giants. He played a couple of seasons for them and, as I discover from my favorite reference book, he was not nearly so good a batter as his son is a poet.

are the chess players. Their players are the pieces
and pawns, whom they move, direct, and remove.
The smallest detail of strategy can win or lose. This
analogy between baseball and chess is an interesting
one. It is especially so because it is so full of holes.
For instance, if you are a chess player, you move
your Queen to King Bishop 5. It may not be the
wisest move but you move her. At the next critical
moment she doesn't get the sun in her eyes and lose
sight of the ball, or get her two feet tangled up with
each other and fall flat on her face. But in the case
of the baseball manager something like that happens not so infrequently. Whether the manager was
smart or dumb becomes a debatable point. It is in-
deed hotly debated most of the cold winter around
the legendary hot stove in the grocery store.

The baseball records are endless. Many of them
are thrilling and many are annoying, sought out by
a newspaperman or broadcaster when he can't think
of anything else to bring up. The latter lean toward
this type of history: That this is the first time on the
opening day in Washington, when the President of
the United States threw out the first ball, that the
losing team scored ten runs.

At the other end, the most glowing statistic in all

baseball, and the most familiar to both bright and stupid people, is that Babe Ruth hit sixty home runs in 1927. A runner-up to this unimaginable success story is that Joe DiMaggio hit safely in fifty-six consecutive games in 1941. Another is that Lou Gehrig never missed a game for 2130 performances. This one, like some other records, is slightly smudged around the cuffs, because even Gehrig sometimes didn't feel well and played a very few innings just to keep his record going. Another less interesting statistic, just coined, is that all these men were Yankees, and that Everett "Deacon" Scott, the shortstop who previously held the record for playing every game, was also a Yankee.

A few years ago it was suggested that the playing season be made a little longer than the historic 154 games. According to this classic arrangement each of the eight clubs plays each of the others twenty-two times, eleven at home and eleven away. The modest proposal was for each team to play one more game against each other team. The basic idea was one usually applauded in our country—to make more money for everybody. The suggestion came from the "Magnates." (In case anyone doesn't know, the Magnates are the bad guys. The players,

and the public, and everyone else, except perhaps some umpires, are the good guys.)

This reasonable request to try and make a little more dough was howled down by practically everybody. This was not because anyone was opposed to making more money, or even seeing someone else, like the Magnates, do it. The overwhelming objection was that it would invalidate the records which had all been predicated on the same number of big-league games per season. Not just the Babe's unforgettable accomplishment, but all the other records too, most strike-outs, double plays, errors, stolen bases, and stolen towels. The archivists won out, and nearly everyone heaved a sigh of relief. Thus the fan, when he saw something unusual at a game he happened to attend, could still look it up and have the pleasure of finding out just how unusual it was.

Unusualness is one of the prime charms of big-league baseball. As observed before, when you buy a ticket you do not know whether or not you are purchasing an unforgettable experience or just an afternoon in the fresh air.

Take the matter of the no-hit game. There are three categories and anyone who has ever seen any of them will be glad to tell you all about it, any time. There is the "almost" no hitter, the no hitter, and the "perfect" no hitter. The almost no hitter is unusual enough. A pitcher goes, say, seven full innings without giving a hit. Everybody knows this and nobody is supposed to mention it, because it will put the "whammy" on the pitcher. Most players and fans are superstitious and many of them are just stupid. Anyway, in the eighth, or worse yet the ninth, somebody gets a hit. This reproduces the qualities of a Greek tragedy.

A no hitter is a game with one team making no hits, as you perhaps have already guessed. It happens one or two or three times a season, and more frequently no times a season. The no hitter is *much* more unusual than the almost.

A perfect no hitter I do not think you personally are ever going to see. But then of course you might. A perfect is when no one gets to first base for any reason such as base on balls, or even a fielding error. Of course an error is not the pitcher's fault (unless he makes it himself) but still it is not a perfect no hitter. Since the turn of the century there have been over sixty thousand big-league games pitched (and with two starting pitchers to each game, making

*. . . everybody in the country is praying for
the pitcher . . .*

over one hundred twenty thousand opportunities)
and only four perfect ones. (So far, that is.) Of
those four, one is still in dispute on technical
grounds.*

* The legal aspects of this one require the services of a
Solomon. The game also includes Babe Ruth, who as you will
shortly see was included in many events besides home runs.
The Babe was then a wonderful pitcher for Boston. He
started this game in 1917 and the umpire said that he walked
the first batter. The Babe disagreed so pungently that the
ump tossed him out of the game. Then a pretty fair pitcher
named Ernie Shore took his place without, one presumes,
much time for a warm-up. The man on first tried stealing

When a no hitter seems possible, everybody in the country is praying for the pitcher with the possible exception of the opposing team. The only event that surpasses this in spiritual intensity is waiting for Armistice Day. Now it is simple enough to see why a whole country prays for peace, but why should a whole country pray, for thirty minutes, for a no hitter?

The best answer I have found is in a highbrow

---

and was thrown out. Of the next twenty-six batters to face Shore, none reached first base. How do you call it, Solomon?

book whose author perhaps has no interest in baseball whatever. It is called *The Dark Voyage and
the Golden Mean*, by Albert Cook (Harvard University Press). The leading theme I shall try to ex-
press in my words, not Professor Cook's:

In the pattern of living there are two opposites.
They are the Wonderful and the Probable. Everyone is yearning for the Wonderful, but the Probable is what most of us nearly always get. Something Wonderful happens to each of us once in a
while but not nearly often enough. Only a handful
of people do something decisive with their lives in
an effort to seek the Wonderful. Among such are
saints, criminals, poets, and hoboes. For the rest of
us the Probable keeps happening pretty probably.
The sun rises each day in the east and a couple of
hours later the commuting train takes us to the
south, and the same conductor punches our ticket,
and so forth.

Of the people at a ball game only a tiny percentage are saints or criminals. For the rest of us, a
no hitter, of no intrinsic importance, is yet truly
Wonderful.* It seldom happens. And here we are,

* While we are discussing the occasional appearance of the
Wonderful, or the Unlikely, here is a small example: The

a part of it, rooting the pitcher home!

I have seen only one triple play in my life. This was not televised, but the trouble is I didn't quite see it. It was at a dull spring training game in Florida. There were men at first and second and none out. My companion was Arthur Mann, the baseball historian. I had turned to him to impart some of my

---

material above was first researched and then typed out only one or two weeks before Monday, October 8, 1956, a day that will not soon be forgotten.

That day dawned sunny and pleasant and about eleven o'clock, after reading the sports page, I phoned a neighbor who knows practically everything about everything, but extremely little about baseball. "How would you like to drive down to New York with me and see a World Series game?" I asked. "I am willing to explain the game to you as it unfolds."

He said, "That would be great, but can we get in?"

"Certainly we can get in. It is the fifth game, the least alluring of a Series; it is a Monday, and the Yankee Stadium has about a million seats," I explained. "Oh, I see," he said gratefully.

So we drove forty miles, parked the car in anguish, and found there was standing room only. I weigh a lot and have flat feet.

"Oh, let's go home," I said disgustedly, "I have seen World Series games before."

"Yes," he said, "but I haven't." And he insisted on herding me in.

wisdom or to ask some dumb question. There was the crack of the bat and in two seconds three men were out. The part I saw of it was the last second where the second baseman tossed the ball to the first baseman. I suppose if I had been at Waterloo I would have been reading a detective story.

---

It wasn't even good standing room, but it was some performance. The standee who was blocking our view most effectively was a large French Canadian from Montreal, where Jackie Robinson first bloomed. He was naturally all for the Dodgers.

Along about the sixth, the big Canuck turned around to my friend and me, and said doubtfully, "You know, I think I will root for this perfect game. Then I can tell them in Montreal, 'I was there.'" He was clearly asking us to pass on a question of ethics. My friend said, "It is perfectly all right for you to do that. And if the perfect game comes off we will give you a signed affidavit that you were there."

As all the world knows, it came off. My feet hurt but otherwise I felt as good as Don Larsen. During the last innings eighty thousand people screamed at every out and finally at every pitch, unless it was a ball.

I am informed by a knowledgeable friend that during those innings the most apprehensive person present was not Larsen. It was the three official scorers. Had there been any kind of bobble the scorers would have had the responsibility of calling it a hit or an error, and wiping a perfect game from the records. This point is discussed generally in Chapter Six.

The most unusual thing I ever saw was also not televised and I wish I had never seen it, and so did the other twenty thousand present. I was a youngster and my brother beside me was younger. Yankee pitcher Carl Mays let go one of his underhand slants and it hit Cleveland shortstop Chapman on the temple. Neither my brother nor I suspected we had seen something dreadful happen. Neither did at least one Yankee infielder. There was a sound, just the same as would be made by a bunt and the ball bounced fair and this infielder acting on long-established instinct fielded it cleanly and threw to first. Chapman slowly sat down. It was not until the plate umpire dropped to one knee, took Chapman's shoulder in his hands and peered into his eyes that the crowd began to realize that this was no routine "hit by pitcher." He died the next day.

Mays went on to have some great seasons. In my youth I just thought that this was sort of unfair. I now realize that it wasn't entirely because he was a good pitcher; part of it was that batters remembered what had happened once. Of course he had no more desire to "kill" anyone than you or I have.

Baseball has been described in an article by Roger Angell as "The Perfect Game," and the title is very well proved. However, in my opinion the game is not quite perfect. It has one ugly flaw; there is an effective advantage to be gained by a dangerous procedure, which is to throw a fast ball as close to a batter's nose as possible. Some pitchers do this and some would not think of doing it. The umpires are sometimes angry, sometimes disgusted, but there is little they can do about it. Like most other forms of Sin, it is difficult to legislate about.

There is a bright spot to add to this gloomy "statistic" about Chapman. It is most likely that such a tragedy will never happen again. Players have finally been persuaded to wear protective caps while batting. Say what you will about ball players, they are generally a rather boyish lot. It took a generation since Chapman's time to persuade them to do this simple thing. It hurt their manly pride. They were always willing to protect their meat hand with a glove and their shins with a guard and their digestions with patent medicines. But to protect themselves from sudden and undeserved death in their prime, that was asking too much. That would be womanish.

I will conclude this with my own personal favorite baseball statistic. I doubt if it is anyone else's.

Ruth's sixty homers is a glorious statistic but it is not quite my favorite. That was accomplished by skill and power and courage. Almost any genius in any line can do something like that.

The statistic I find fascinating was accomplished by a first baseman, Rip Collins, who operated for the Cubs in the middle thirties. What do you guess Collins did one afternoon? Hit four home runs? No. That would not have been an enormous distinction because several men have done it in the game's history. So what did Collins do?

Remember he played first base. In most games the first baseman makes more of the putouts than the other eight positions together. All the rest of the infield throw the ball to him to retire the batter when that is feasible, which it mostly is. He also frequently catches balls both fair and foul. He usually makes an assist or two, picking up a grounder and for strategic reasons throwing it to another base, or to home.

Well, perhaps you have guessed it. If you have any mathematical sense perhaps you won't believe it. But on that afternoon (it has never happened since) Collins played his position for nine innings and never got his hands on the ball. He had no

*. . . he could have fielded his position lying down
on his stomach . . .*

"official chances." Nobody threw the ball to him
and nobody batted one to him. This was not because he was unpopular; it just happened that way.
The only times he touched the ball were when
they tossed it around the infield for pepping up in
between outs, all of which outs were made by his
companions. If he could have known what was

going to happen he could have fielded his position
lying down on his stomach or sitting on the bench
and only entering the contest when it was his turn
to bat. Defensively it would have made no difference.

This miracle of Collins will only be of interest
to those who are interested in the wonderful science
of mathematical probabilities.

This science tells us that no matter how improb-
able an event is it will become probable if the
"sampling" is large and long enough. (In major
league baseball, the proper sampling runs from
about the beginning of the twentieth century, when
accurate records began to be kept. This makes the
sampling, for the two leagues, approach seventy
thousand games to date.)

Here is an experiment in probabilities requir-
ing little apparatus save patience. Take a coin out
of your pocket and attempt to flip it heads ten times
in succession. It doesn't matter who you are or
where you are, or what are your abilities. The
chances are you will not do well in this attempt. To
be accurately discouraging about it, the chances
against you are a little more than a thousand to one
for the first time you try it. The odds are just as

bad the second time you try, and also for the third and all the rest of the times.

This fact is more or less familiar to a lot of people. But a lot of people are not at all familiar with this: If you will take your coin and plan to flip it about ten thousand times, it is a thousand to one that at some point of this dreary exercise you *will* flip ten heads in succession. In other words it would be next to impossible to *avoid* performing a miracle. You just need a large enough sampling.

Collins is the ultimate in the occasional triumph of the Wonderful over the Probable. The cool voice of mathematics explains to us why it happened. Equally coldly the same voice predicts that some day it will happen again to some other first baseman, but it doesn't say when.

Some day, in the twelfth inning of a nothing to nothing tie game, a pitcher with a lifetime batting average of .143, who has never hit a home run in his ten-year career, will break up that game with a home run.

Experienced baseball men may doubt this but no mathematician will.

# CHAPTER SIX

# The Box Score and Other Minutiae

---

*Time is of the essence. The shadow moves*
*From the plate to the box, from the box to second base,*
*From second to the outfield, to the bleachers.*

Consider a not unfamiliar afternoon. It is a miserable afternoon, too hot, or too cool, and also too windy. The two poorest teams in the league are playing a meaningless contest late in the season. There are less than a thousand spectators. In the vast stands they appear rarer than raisins in the most disappointing raisin bun, and half of them haven't paid their way in. And among those who haven't paid for tickets is the official scorer. He will pay strict attention, even though no one else does, even though one team makes seven runs in the first inning alone, and the other team finally makes one in the last half of the eighth.

He will note down, ineluctably and accurately, everything. All the triumphs and all the disasters.

After that he will not airily toss away his notes, as most fans chuck away their carefully kept score cards. Far from it. The next day, through publishing devices as complex as New York Stock Exchange transactions require, his notes will appear in hundreds of newspapers all over the land. True they will engage less than six square inches of type; they will be intensely abbreviated, and cryptic. They will then become the "box scores." Only the sophisticated will be able to decipher them. The number of people with the special knowledge to do this is limited, on this continent, to a bare forty or fifty million.

This game being so insignificant, it is likely that no more than half a million newspaper readers took the trouble to notice that Celewiskey, the new third baseman for the losing team, made three errors and did not improve matters by coming to bat four times and making no hits. If it had been a World Series game, fifty million readers would have studied the box score. (For a Series game, the box score is printed in much bigger type because a lot of baseball illiterates will be trying to decipher it. Several millions of them, examining this type of information for the first time, will learn to understand it. They will become members of a huge scholarly society—the habitual studiers of box scores.)

The baseball box score is the pithiest form of written communication in America today. It is abbreviated history. It is two or three hours (the box score even gives *that* item to the minute) of complex activity, virtually inscribed on the head of a pin, yet no knowing reader suffers from eyestrain. If you know how to read a box score completely you can pretty well find out what happened without reading the lyric sentences that precede it.

The box score, for brevity, is to the *Reader's Digest* what the *Reader's Digest* is to a book titled *Primary Trends in Modern Retail Merchandising.* The box score also has many times the readers of the *Reader's Digest,* which of course has more readers than anything else.

In a box score nearly everything is abbreviated except the remorseless numerals. The hapless Celewiskey, for example, on perhaps the only day in his life when he got his name (and his shame) into several hundred metropolitan newspapers, finds himself referred to as "Cel'sky, 3b." But under H, it says clearly enough "O" and under E it says "3." This deplorable biography, for anyone who is interested, will be available for reference until the day before Judgment Day. "You Could Look It Up."* as James Thurber titled one of the best of fantasy baseball stories.

This chapter is not going to explain what each of the abbreviations, a few of them quite puzzling, mean. To do so would be entirely wrong, just as it would be wrong to produce a didactic piece explaining to young men how to whistle at young women. If you don't know how to do it, but wish to learn, you should learn by yourself, not read up on it in the public library. If by chance you do not

---

* The place to look this up, or anything else up, is in *The Official Encyclopedia of Baseball*, by Hy Turkin and S. C. Thompson (New York: A. S. Barnes & Co., rev. ed., 1956). There is also an inexpensive pocket edition, but I prefer to consult the one that weighs several pounds.

*. . . but be sure he knows the answers . . .*

know how to read a box score, just start studying
some box scores. If you are a boy I do not think
you should ask anyone for help, except perhaps
your father. (It will tickle your old man, but be

sure he knows the answers before you ask him.) If you are a girl you may ask any man, if you choose. But this is the easy way, and also the flirtatious way.

The first thing you must do, and practically the last, is to procure a copy of a metropolitan newspaper, turn to the sports section, select a box score, and gaze at it. The form differs a little from paper to paper. *The New York Times*, as usual, is perhaps the most explicit. Reading in the usual order, the abbreviations at the top mean at bats, runs, hits, putouts, assists. Errors are sometimes a sixth column, sometimes underneath, according to the whim of the sports typesetter.

At bats are important because of batting averages. If a man is at bat five times and makes two hits, his batting average for that game is .400. If he is at bat only four times and makes two hits it comes to .500. Such figures are commonplace in box scores, but for the whole season nobody ever bats .500 and the last to bat over .400 was Ted Williams a good many years ago.

It is feasible for an athlete to come up to the plate five times, swinging a big bat, and in the next day's box score have a zero under AB. This would happen, for instance, if he were walked twice, made a sacrifice fly and a sacrifice bunt, and got hit by the pitcher the last time. This may seem kind of ludicrous, but anyone who studies up on batting averages will learn that there is precise justice here, aimed at, and very nearly arrived at. Anyway a lot more precise than Blackstone's *Commentaries*.

The other item worth noting is the chancy field of "errors." Although errors are committed by the fielding side, they have a lot to do with batting averages. (There are such things as fielding averages but no one pays any attention to them.)

The point is, of course, that if a batter hits the ball, and arrives safe at first (or any other base), and the official scorer says an error was committed, the batter does not get credited with a hit, only another accursed time at bat. So what is an error? This has never been entirely satisfactorily settled. It is clearly an error if a ball comes cleanly to a fielder, and he for some reason, perhaps because the sun is in his eyes, perhaps because of marital problems at home, just drops it to the ground. But this obvious type of error does not happen much in big-league ball.

It is the debatable errors which are the scorer's headache. The batter hits a sharp grounder to the right of the shortstop, the more difficult side. The shortstop bobbles it a tiny moment, comes up with it, but cannot pivot and throw fast enough so the batter just beats it out. Now if the shortstop had been Honus Wagner, or even himself five years younger, he would undoubtedly have made the play successfully. What should the scorer call it? Such is the general philosophy of the game that he will probably call it a hit. Sometimes he will call it an error and then the batter will not talk to him for a month. For the batter has been robbed of a hit, and as has often been observed, hits are a ball player's bread and butter. (Exception: they are not normally a pitcher's bread and butter; strikeouts are. Exception to the exception is, as usual, Babe Ruth. He hit so well that he gave up being a pitcher, and then his hits became his little crackers and caviar.)

Batting averages are terribly important to a player's reputation and salary, but fielding averages are scarcely regarded. The reason for this is somewhat curious. Fielding averages are the percentage of errors to chances. But again we must ask, what is an error? Only one thing is sure. A fielder is not charged with an error if he does not touch the ball. This may often happen because the fielder is day-

*All he can be charged with is not being a particularly valuable player.*

dreaming, or is slow of foot, or of mind, or has stationed himself a couple of yards wrong for this batter on this pitch. None of these four things is a recommendation for a ball player. But if he doesn't manage to touch the ball he cannot, under anybody's scoring rules, be charged with an error. All he can be charged with is not being a particularly valuable ball player. A speedy, heads-up player can get to difficult balls, grab at them, almost have them, and muff them. So it is the good fielder who gives himself extra chances to make errors. That is why good managers and knowledgeable fans do not give a hoot if a fielder's average is .992 or .981.

Runs batted in (RBI) is an important statistic, and it has puzzling aspects. It is not unusual to find that a .310 batter has batted in only fifty runs in the season, while a .270 hitter has batted in about a hundred. This can be accounted for in many ways, none of them necessarily correct. It may be as simple a matter as being first man up. First man up has no opportunity in the first inning to bat in anybody but himself. (A home run counts as batting yourself in.) It may be the difference between a long-ball hitter and a "spray" hitter, who is a useful person to have on the team, but who only hits two home runs a year because he is not big and strong enough.

It may have to do with the imponderable matter of whether he is a "clutch" hitter. ("Clutch," in the baseball sense, will not be found in many dictionaries. It is likely a wild aberration on the word "crucial," or "crux," or both.) Certain famous players are renowned for being good in the clutch.

A reasonable view of this matter would be that it doesn't exist. It is reasonable to assume that a professional player would do his best to get a hit every time he comes to bat, regardless of the importance of the situation, or even if the game is only in spring training. If the situation is tremendously important, with fifty thousand bellowing their hopes and fears, he may try even harder. (This may be his undoing.) So one might reason that if he can get one of his hits in a crucial situation, swell! If he can't, that is too bad, but after all, he has also failed to hit in thousands of unimportant situations. The average player gets only one hit in three times or four times.

However, this rational view is not a correct view. The records do not show it with any precision, but there are such things as clutch hitters, and there are other hitters with high batting averages who are

*There are, however, other men who secretly would rather be elsewhere.*

pretty dismal in the clutch. The usual conclusion about this is that the clutch hitters have courage, or guts, or intestinal fortitude. My own theory varies somewhat.

I think it is a matter of temperament. There are some men who mightily enjoy being in the eye of a hurricane; they enjoy it even more if the whole world is watching. On such occasions their red corpuscles go racing around joyously inside of them. They would rather be up there with the bases full, two out, and big money riding on the next pitch, than anywhere else in the world. (Ruth was one such.) There are, however, other men who secretly would rather be elsewhere. Is it correct to call such men yellow? Or is it perhaps to call the brave men eager exhibitionists? There is a record that baseball does not and cannot keep: Of the clutch hitters who can look a skillful pitcher in the eye, how many of them can look other critical situations in life in the eye? But it is not a statistic I want to see added to the box score.

The box score is full of little curiosities, if you have the eagerness to hunt them out. Take this runs batted in business. It seems simple enough. But not always. If you are at bat and you hit a fly that is caught, or a foul even that is caught, and there is a man on third who "tags up" and scores, then even though you are out you get credit for an RBI. You can also "bat in" a run without striking the ball at all. The bases are full and you get a base on balls. Perhaps you never even hit a foul, or even took the bat off your shoulder.

At first glance this seems unfair. A little old lady could do the same thing. Maybe she could, and maybe she couldn't, especially if she happened to be an over-eager old lady as many of them are. It takes a good eye and good judgment to get a base on balls with the bases loaded.

The other reason why this scoring law exists is more practical and has less to do with blindfolded justice. A box score must "prove" like double-entry bookkeeping. Every run must be accounted for and so must everything else. A run has been scored. Who batted it in? What more likely candidate than the batter who didn't do any batting? Whom would you suggest—the third-base coach who signalled him to "wait the pitcher out"? That might be correct but it happens that neither the coaches' nor the managers' names ever appear in the box score.

On the defensive side, the bookkeeping is no less severe. Sometimes when the umpire calls "infield fly" no infielder bothers to catch the high short pop-up and it falls to the ground. Yet the runner is automatically out. Who put him out? The scoring rules state that it is the infielder who was nearest to the ball. This might appear to be a picayune ruling, but it isn't. When a team takes the field for nine full innings, the total of putouts must be twenty-seven. (Nine times three equals twenty-seven.) So some fielder must be given that putout or the box score will not prove.

When I was a lad the "infield fly rule" was discussed as much as the high and low tariff. By this time most fans have gotten accustomed to it, and understand its peculiar necessity.

The game of baseball was played for generations without any need for so unnatural a rule as the infield fly. Then a thought occurred to one player— I believe it was that intellectual second baseman Eddie Collins. Lying sleepless one night in, I like to think, an alien hotel room (and in those days a bum one) he reviewed in his remarkable mind a familiar situation. There are runners on first and second and less than two out. The batter hits an easy pop-up to him and he easily catches it. The two runners do not move or even consider doing so. The batter is out. That is the way this routine play has been enacted for three quarters of a century. One man, and only one man, out.

But tossing on his thin, not too clean mattress, I like to think, he suddenly gets an inspiration worthy of Tom Watt. "Eureka," he cries to himself, "suppose I don't catch it? Suppose I drop it on purpose? Then the force is on both runners. I pick up the ball and throw to third and the third baseman throws to second. The batter gets safe to first, but *two* men are out. I've made the easiest double play in history."

He was of course absolutely right in his strategy. The runners are helpless if this is perpetrated on them. The very next day, I like to think, he tried out this caper with stunning success and all the Solons in baseball looked at each other in dismay. They finally solved it with a peculiarly unnatural rule. When a pop fly is hit up under certain conditions, the umpire yells, "infield fly." Then the batter is automatically out. The infielder nearest the ball may catch it if he enjoys catching flys (he usually does, especially at a time like this when there is nothing at stake), but if he wishes to he can disdain even reaching for the ball. The batter is just as out as if he had either caught it or muffed it.*

If you make a daily habit, not just a World Series habit, of studying box scores you will find all sorts of nuances in them (if that is the sort of thing that

---

* Further research into this difficult subject seems to show that the history of the rule may not be precisely as I have set it down here. But the precise version, whatever it may be, is probably no more interesting than what I have set down, so what the heck.

interests you). For instance, the very last item is the attendance. When there is a double header, it only gives the attendance for the first game. It assumes that nobody got up and went home before the second game. When each team uses more than one pitcher it gives the winning and losing pitcher (WP and LP). But when a pitcher pitches the whole game this item is omitted. It is redundant, and some dozen letters of type are saved.

When a succession of pitchers are used the question of who is the WP and who the LP sometimes comes up, sometimes practically unsolvably. In a majority of games a child could make the pronouncement, but not in all.

If you want to know the exact legislation on this point, get any rule book, or better and less expensive, ask an old-time fan. He will tell you a lot of stuff about (when a new pitcher comes in) that it is the new pitcher's game "to win or lose" according to the score at the moment of his baptism into the lineup. This is all quite right.

But in one of those dipsy-dopsey games, where each team uses above five pitchers, and the final score is 14-11, and nobody pitches well, and nobody pitches perceptibly worse than anyone else, the case is different. Nobody really deserves to be credited WP, and nobody should be assigned LP. Every-body pitched just lousy.

But the records are sacrosanct, as they should be. If a game is won, there must be a winning pitcher to account for it, and vice versa. To award this laurel and this badge of shame, it would be accepta-ble to examine the entrails of a sacramental goat, as the Greek soothsayers did. Actually this practice is still occasionally used, without the goat.

There are a good many cases where the winning pitcher only threw one ball. He came in with his team behind and a man or so on base. He threw his one ball, which resulted in a double or triple play, and the side was retired. Then he was lifted for a pinch hitter, went and took his shower, and his team came on to win. A pitcher who only throws one ball does not seem a likely candidate for WP, but who seems more likely, since everyone who came after him did nothing so effective?

It is possible to dream up a case of a winning pitcher who never threw a pitch at all. He comes in with men on base and two out. His first throw (not a pitch) is to a baseman and he picks a runner off.*

---

* I don't know if this ever happened. I am not going to bother to look it up either.

You can make a daily habit of studying your favorite team's box score *before* you read the thrilling account in prose that goes above it. You will eventually get so proficient at this that you can pretty well find out what happened in the prose recital. Of course you can't go all the way. You can tell if a batter was hit by a pitcher and who they both were, but you cannot find out how badly the batter was hurt. This kind of early morning doodling I find in the class of crossword puzzles and daily bridge problems. One more bit of advice: If you try this little recreation out, and find you don't care for it, just give it up.

The matter of keeping score on the scorecard that you purchase is another thing you should not do if you do not enjoy doing it. Millions of people just love it; they had a distant ancestor who was a bookkeeper.

A friend of mine name of Rudyard Kipling once remarked:

*There are nine and sixty ways of constructing tribal lays,*
*And each and every one of them is right.*

This is also true of keeping score. You can keep

it the right way, whatever that is, or any of the other sixty-eight ways. If you are a perfectionist you will only find peace of mind by keeping it the right way, but if you are a perfectionist you already know how to do it better than I do. For instance, it is customary, when a batter strikes out, to put the letter "K" in the appropriate little box. Why it is K, instead of S, I shall never know until some stranger writes me a sharply worded letter explaining it. I often go to games with a perfectionist friend of mine, a former professional ball reporter. He puts the K in all right when the batter strikes out swinging, but when the batter just stands there with the bat on his shoulder for the third strike, looking silly, my friend prints the K in backwards, as it appears in a mirror. Actually a lot of other scorers do this also, but do not count me among them.

After the meticulous scorers have done all this they usually throw the score card away. Occasionally, if it has been a memorable game, they take the card home with them, put it carefully away somewhere, and never look at it again for the rest of their lives. It is hard for me to imagine anyone, on a frosty December evening, sitting before the fire

*. . . a pretty profound character . . .*

with the score card of a game played the previous June, and recreating the game, batter by batter and inning by inning. However it has undoubtedly happened. In baseball, as has been mentioned before, everything eventually happens. Another thing I can't imagine is a wife saying to her husband as he departs for the game without her, "Be sure to bring back your score card, dear, I want to read it."

The genuine reason for the nonprofessional

scorer keeping score is for the period of the game itself. It will allow you to note, toward the end of the game, that the batter coming up has struck out all three times before, once swinging. Better yet, you can speak up and give this information to the people sitting near you, who will consider you a pretty profound character, which as it happens, you are.

In order to keep score, you must assign a number to each player. The pitcher is 1, and the right fielder is 9. First be sure to underline the starting pitchers and catchers when the batteries are announced over the loud speaker. Underline them firmly. This may break the point in the lead pencil you just purchased for five cents. Since you don't happen to have a pencil sharpener in your pocket, you can no longer keep score, but will just have to sit back and enjoy the old ball game. Don't be downhearted; if there are points of very recent history you want to know there will be plenty of score keepers about who will be happy to inform you.

# CHAPTER SEVEN

# The Armchair versus the Hard Wooden Seat

---

*Time is of the essence. The crowd and players*
*Are the same age always, but the man in the crowd*
*Is older every season. Come on, play ball!*

The lines above are the end of the poem. I have always thought that they were beautiful and melancholy, and a profound statement about two important subjects: Baseball and Life.

There are many people who do not care for baseball at all, either for playing, watching, discussing,

*These people are well within their rights.*

or reading about. These people are well within their rights. (I do not care for grand opera; no one has been mean to me because of this. I think it would have been better for me if I had been able to enjoy grand opera. Too late now, I am growing older every opera season.)

But there are plenty of people who like baseball

and are willing to do something about it beyond just turning on a switch and lolling in their own living room with a can of beer. They are not only willing to buy a ticket, they are willing to do something more important, which is to contribute some of their own energies. It is not the easiest thing, physically, to attend a game, especially a standout game. It is true that in Detroit a patron of the game can saunter airily from the Book-Cadillac Hotel and soon stroll into the Stadium, but in other cities he has to do more work. Even in Detroit, however, you will find as in all other parks that boys are constantly trying to sell you hot dogs when you are not hungry, and that you cannot find those boys when you get hungry. But if you are watching TV at home you can, whenever you like, have any sort of midsummer delicacies served by your wife, if you have a wife who is willing to do all this, and who also knows how to construct delicacies.

I do not intend to be very harsh with TV baseball watching. One reason is that even if I were harsh, I don't think the beer and razor blade people would throw up their hands and say to each other, "Let's quit." Also, I often look at baseball myself in my living room, and sometimes in a bar. When it it a poor game I can turn it off without any feeling of being gypped of time or money.

When it is a fine game, though, I feel I have missed something by not going out to the park. In a real ball park on a lively day there are so many more interesting and exciting things to watch than can be seen on TV. The folks, the fun, the flags . . . By the way, how many in the class know that the flags, or pennants, of the various eight cities which flutter at the roof of the grandstand are accurately arranged each day in order of the standing of the clubs in the race at that moment?

The television people, for reasons of subtle business policy, also urge the viewer to get out to the old ball park. However, they urge him half heartedly, or anyway three quarters heartedly. They do not make full use of their vast arsenal of talent and imagination. For instance, no announcer has as yet put his plea this way:

"Tomorrow Boston comes into town for a crucial three-day series. Go to the park and enjoy the game; there are more than ten thousand seats still available. If you go to the game, the air will be fresher than it is where you now are! And here is another point for a thoughtful fan to consider. If

*A faraway technician has his hands tightly on
your head . . .*

you actually go to the game, you will not be re-
quired, every ten minutes, to view and listen to,
eighteen commercials that you have witnessed ten
thousand times before."

The habitual watching of baseball in the parlor,
instead of the park, is not a crime, or even a minor
vice, but it comes somewhere after that. My sug-

gested demurrers to TV ball are first practical, and second vaguely "moral."

The practical matter *is* that if you are a really interested fan you don't quite see the game on TV. A faraway technician has his hands tightly on your head and your eyeballs. He is in charge of what you look at. He is far from unintelligent but he can't cater to your special interests. When Willie Mays is chasing a desperate fly he will show you Mays chasing it. If you were at the park you would also watch Mays, but you might take a moment off for a quick glance to see if the base runners were tagging up or running, which is a delicate matter of tactics. You might want to glance at how the infield is shaping up for the relay, or a dozen other things. But when you are sitting in an upholstered chair, instead of a not-so-comfortable wooden bench, you will see what the cameraman decides you shall see. You will miss a lot. This of course includes catching cold, if there should be a sudden downpour.

As to the "moral" angle, my objection is that to enjoy a fine experience, such as a splendid ball game, by languidly turning a dial is just a little too easy, a little too lazy. I would not care to defend this Puritanical notion in open court with a lot of hecklers about, but I am sure there are some who rather agree.

Here is a further suggestion on the point: It has been observed that a baseball lover sometimes recalls in reverie the details of a thrilling play he saw long ago. It is my suggestion that such pleasant memories are always of plays seen at the park, not slouched before a TV set. There just seems to be nothing memorable about a great game seen on television.

It reminds me of an argument I once heard about the relative merits, or demerits, of drinking hard liquor and smoking cigarettes. One of our party, a cigarette smoker and a whiskey drinker, was particularly incensed at cigarette smoking. We asked him what he was so sore about. He explained, "Cigarettes do me at least as much harm as whiskey, but I have never had any memorable adventures as a result of a couple of packs of Camels."

Early in this century the philosopher William James initiated a search for what he called a "moral equivalent of war." (Didn't find it.) I think we all know more or less what he was driving at, whether we recall this then famous essay or not. It was a search for a large activity, into which an individual plunges himself with a sense of noble and passionate purpose, with a vast concourse of his fellows. This activity should offer excitement, dedication, and partisanship, which is what a war offers, or seems to offer, the youth of a nation. Now if it is suggested that to be one of a vast number of passionate baseball fans is a moral equivalent of war, I admit that this is too big an order to swallow. And yet it is as good an equivalent as any other I can think of, except, perhaps, for music (which is international, has more devotees, and also has not prevented several wars.)

However, this notion that sports, and the arts, may be a possible moral equivalent is not perhaps so foolish as may first appear. We have had several wars in this generation. Without sports and the arts we might have had several more. Mr. George F. Kennan* has shrewdly observed that among the many causes of war, boredom ranks high. Let it be understood that when baseball is proposed as a possible moral equivalent, we are talking about watching baseball from a hard wooden bench, with the

* *American Diplomacy, 1900-1950*, (Chicago: University of Chicago Press, 1951).

folks all around you, and not from an armchair with
a pal or two.

I will conclude with a true anecdote. I set it down
as one example of the many pleasant little things
that can happen in a grandstand but not in the living
room.

I know a man who, as a little boy, used to be
taken out to the ball park by his father. At a certain
point in the game the father would say to his son:

"Pretty soon now I am going to pass my miracle."

"What is the miracle, Pop?" his son would ask
eagerly.

"I will put two fingers in my mouth and whistle.
Then nearly all the people here will stand up."

After the miracle had come off pretty well in
the seventh inning, the little boy would ask,

"Why didn't they all of them stand up?"

"I'm not that good at miracles."

# Polo·Grounds

*by Rolfe Humphries*

*Time is of the essence. This is a highly skilled*
*And beautiful mystery. Three or four seconds only*
*From the time that Riggs connects till he reaches first,*
*And in those seconds Jurges goes to his right,*
*Comes up with the ball, tosses to Witek at second*
*For the force on Reese, Witek to Mize at first,*
*In time for the out—a double play.*

*(Red Barber crescendo. Crowd noises, obbligato;*
*Scattered staccatos from the peanut boys,*
*Loud in the lull, as the teams are changing sides) . . .*

*Hubbell takes the sign, nods, pumps, delivers—*
*A foul into the stands. Dunn takes a new ball out,*
*Hands it to Danning, who throws it down to Werber;*
*Werber takes off his glove, rubs the ball briefly,*
*Tosses it over to Hub, who goes to the rosin bag,*
*Takes the sign from Danning, pumps, delivers,*
*Low, outside, ball three. Danning goes to the mound,*
*Says something to Hub, Dunn brushes off the plate,*
*Adams starts throwing in the Giant bullpen,*
*Hub takes the sign from Danning, pumps, delivers,*
*Camilli gets hold of it, a long fly to the outfield,*
*Ott goes back, back, back, against the wall, gets under*
     *it,*
*Pounds his glove, and takes it for the out.*
*That's all for the Dodgers. . . .*

*Time is of the essence. The rhythms break,*
*More varied and subtle than any kind of dance;*
*Movement speeds up or lags. The ball goes out*
*In sharp and angular drives, or long, slow arcs,*
*Comes in again controlled and under aim;*
*The players wheel or spurt, race, stoop, slide, halt,*
*Shift imperceptibly to new positions,*
*Watching the signs, according to the batter,*
*The score, the inning. Time is of the essence.*
*Time is of the essence. Remember Terry?*

*Remember Stonewall Jackson, Lindstrom, Frisch,*
*When they were good? Remember long George*
    *Kelly?*
*Remember John McGraw and Benny Kauff?*
*Remember Bridwell, Tenney, Merkle, Youngs,*
*Chief Meyers, Big Jeff Tesreau, Shufflin' Phil?*
*Remember Mathewson, and Ames, and Donlin,*
*Buck Ewing, Rusie, Smiling Mickey Welch?*
*Remember a left-handed catcher named Jack*
    *Humphries,*
*Who sometimes played the outfield, in '83?*

*Time is of the essence. The shadow moves*
*From the plate to the box, from the box to second base,*
*From second to the outfield, to the bleachers.*

*Time is of the essence. The crowd and the players*
*Are the same age always, but the man in the crowd*
*Is older every season. Come on, play ball!*

I thank the generosity of the following experts and non-experts for their suggestions and corrections:

Charles Einstein, Walter J. Fried, Mark Harris, Crockett Johnson, Arthur Mann, Hermine I. Popper, Peter Schwed, Frank Slocum, Joseph A. Thomas, and John R. Tunis.

On second thought, the generosity of these good people is less important than their accuracy. As for my wife, Harriet W. Schwed, she "did nothing in particular, but did it very well."

F. S., Jr.

A NOTE ON THE TYPE IN WHICH THIS BOOK IS SET

*This book was set in Campanella Bold, a type invented about 1948. It is universally admired for its serviceability and plump beauty. It is a very fine type type.*